Ethics of Food

Farming

Vegetables

and Grains

urgan

Heinemann Library
Chicago, Illinois

www.heinemannraintree.com
Visit our website to find out
more information about
Heinemann-Raintree books.

To order:
☎ Phone 888-454-2279
🖥 Visit www.heinemannraintree.com
to browse our catalog and order online.

Edited by Adam Miller, Andrew Farrow, and Adrian
Vigliano
Designed by Ryan Frieson
Illustrated by Mapping Specialists, Ltd. and
Planman Technologies
Picture research by Tracy Cummins
Originated by Capstone Global Library Ltd.
Printed and bound in the United States of America
by Corporate Graphics in North Mankato,
Minnesota
15 14 13 12 11
10 9 8 7 6 5 4 3 2 1

**Library of Congress Cataloging-in-Publication
Data**
Cataloging-in-Publication data is on file at the
Library of Congress.

ISBN 978-1-4329-5100-9 (HB)
ISBN 978-1-4329-6190-9 (PB)

Acknowledgements

The author and publisher are grateful to the
following for permission to reproduce copyright
material: AP Photo pp. 20 (Victor Ruiz C), 34
(Elaine Thompson); Corbis pp. 28 (© Stringer/
Indonesia/Reuters), 37 (© Peter Newcomb/Reuters);
Getty Images pp. 7 (De Agostini Picture Library),
10 (SSPL), 11 (SSPL), 19 (Alfred Eisenstaedt/Time
Life Pictures), 22 (Pankaj Tiwari/The India Today
Group), 41 (AFP PHOTO/ALBERTO PIZZOLI);
istockphoto p. 27 (© luoman); Photo Researchers,
Inc. p. 42 (Lawrence Lawry); Shutterstock pp.
5 (© Supri Suharjoto), 12 (© Jeremy Richards),
15 (© phloem), 16 (© David Kay), 31 (©
dutourdumonde), 38 (© Ruslan Nabiyev), 46 (©
Tish1), 48 (© Maridav).

Cover photograph of corn being grown for biofuel
reproduced with permission of Getty Images (Dave
Reede).

We would like to thank Christopher Nicolson for
his invaluable help in the preparation of this book.

Every effort has been made to contact copyright
holders of any material reproduced in this book.
Any omissions will be rectified in subsequent
printings if notice is given to the publisher.

Contents

Some words are printed in bold, **like this**. You can find out what they mean by looking in the glossary.

Taming Nature, Building Civilization

What is the best way to raise the most affordable, nutritious food—without damaging the planet? Should food companies be allowed to pay their workers wages so low that the employees barely have enough money to live on? Is it okay if the low wages mean lower food costs for others? Companies can provide jobs growing certain crops in poor countries, which is good for local people in those countries. But what if the methods used to grow those crops hurt the environment?

People around the globe are asking these and similar questions every day. The issues involve food **ethics**—the moral rights and wrongs surrounding the production and sale of food.

Up until recently these ethical questions rarely arose. For tens of thousands of years, people were mostly only concerned about having enough food for themselves to live day by day. Only in fairly recent times, as you will read in this book, have small numbers of workers been able to provide enough food for almost everyone in a community.

Because of that effort, plant crops—especially grains—have become a key part of the human diet. And that change has had a great impact on society. At the dinner table this means billions of people have more choices about what they eat than ever before. Food is often fresher and more nutritious, too. But at the same time, even in the world's healthiest countries, people go hungry, or they eat too much food with little nutritional value.

As you read this book, think about the ethics of food. What choices can people make to try to provide enough food for everyone, while preserving their health—and the future of the planet?

Finding food sources

Tens of thousands of years ago, when large parts of Europe and North America were covered in ice, bands of hunters followed prey such as mastodons, which were ancient relatives of the modern elephant. Over time, the ice slowly melted. Humans continued to hunt wild **game**, which now lived in the newly created forests, plains, and marshes. Those animals again became food for the people.

Most supermarkets and grocery stores offer shoppers a wide range of fruits and vegetables.

In other parts of the world, which remained free of ice, humans also ate wild animals from both the land and the sea. For extra calories and **nutrients**, people everywhere gathered wild berries, seeds, nuts, and plants. These early humans are sometimes called hunter-gatherers.

Today, some people still hunt in forests and fields for food, while others search for wild berries or mushrooms to add to their meals. But for most people in the Western world—in places like the United States and Europe—food is raised, grown, and **processed** out of their sight. The only hunting and gathering these modern people do takes place in the aisles of the local supermarket.

But before the modern food system could emerge, with its enormous farms and worldwide markets, a huge change took place in how people live, as we will see.

The rise of agriculture

For most of human existence, people followed the early lifestyle of constantly searching for game and gathering the **edible** plant life nearby. The hunter-gatherers improved their tools over time, replacing bones with stone. Eventually people were able to meet all their dietary needs in one area, usually near rivers or other bodies of water. Because of these changes, people ended their roaming lifestyles and began finding single places to settle in. These people began one of the greatest achievements in human history—the development of **agriculture**, or the use of the soil to grow crops and raise livestock.

Scientists and historians have

Theories about the rise of agriculture

During the age of hunter-gatherers, people could not easily move over large areas. As a result, their food supply was limited. For example, hunters might kill all the game in one region, and neighboring tribes might prevent them from moving into new hunting areas. Given these environmental limits, some of the hunters decided they needed a more reliable source of food. Some historians think domestication of crops and livestock began as people sought to overcome the limits of their traditional food supply.

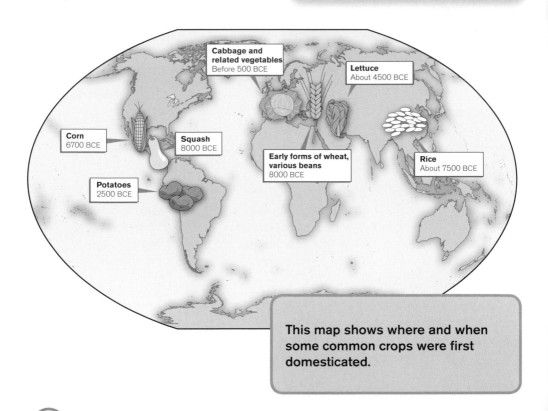

Cabbage and related vegetables
Before 500 BCE

Lettuce
About 4500 BCE

Corn
6700 BCE

Squash
8000 BCE

Early forms of wheat, various beans
8000 BCE

Rice
About 7500 BCE

Potatoes
2500 BCE

This map shows where and when some common crops were first domesticated.

In ancient Egypt, barley and wheat were the two most important grains.

presented many theories to try to explain the rise of agriculture. Why did people begin to take wild seeds, plant them, and raise the crops? No one knows for sure. But the **domestication** (taming for human use) of different plants, especially cereal grains, would have important consequences.

First farmers

Farming began some 12,000 years ago, in a region of southwest Asia called the Fertile Crescent. This area includes parts of modern Iraq, Iran, Syria, Jordan, and Israel. The first crops raised included cereal grains such as barley, rye, and einkorn (a kind of wheat). The edible part of any cereal grain is the seed. The farmers kept some of the seeds to plant their next crop, while using the rest for food. Farmers in Syria also raised lentils, which are plants with edible seeds.

Later, and independently, people in other parts of the world also began to domesticate local crops, with grains becoming an important staple, meaning it was a common food product that people relied upon. In parts of China, farmers grew rice. In Mexico, corn was domesticated. Europeans grew barley and wheat—although historians do not agree if they borrowed agricultural practices or developed farming on their own. But everywhere agriculture rose, the result was the same: the food supply increased. More food meant that a community could support a larger number of people, so **populations** grew.

While some ancient people still hunted and fished for some of their food, the rise of agriculture caused grains to become central to most of the world's diet. They could be easily stored, which meant that a food supply was available all year long. The grains were whole, meaning they were not **refined**, as grains commonly are today. The whole grain has a variety of nutrients important for health. And grains could be fed to livestock, which provided people with protein through the animals' meat or milk.

Birth of civilizations

As some members of the community specialized in farming, others had more time to pursue other activities. Separate classes of people emerged: rulers, priests, warriors, and artists. People also increasingly remained sedentary, meaning they settled in a single spot. They developed greater social interactions with larger circles of people than the hunter-gatherers had. With the rise of agriculture came the first civilizations—political communities based around a major city, with influence that extended beyond its borders.

The first civilizations had governments that collected taxes and paid for skilled artisans to create goods and construct grand public buildings. The earliest forms of writing developed, as governments kept records of finances and laws. As humans settled down to farm, they opened up doors to nation-building, creativity, and wealth—although wealth was not usually shared by everyone in a given civilization. The greatest wealth went to the rulers and their families and favored friends.

The Columbian Exchange

The spread of many foods around the world began in the 15th century, when European explorers began to reach other continents. Italian explorer Christopher Columbus helped begin an exchange of food, as crops he discovered in the Americas soon traveled around the world. At the same time, European and Asian foods were brought to the Americas. The following are some of the crops from this exchange, known as the Columbian Exchange:

Foods brought from the Americas to Europe and Asia	Foods brought from Europe and Asia to the Americas
Maize (corn)	Wheat
Tomato	Barley
Potato	Apple
Cacao (source of chocolate)	Cattle
Vanilla	Soybean
Peanut	Carrot
Chili pepper	Chicken
Blueberry	Sugarcane

Developing agriculture

Raising crops has always been demanding work. People had to clear trees to create areas where they could plant. They had to **harvest** their crops by hand. Farmers used animals to help with the work—for example, an ox might pull a plow or turn the stone that ground grain into flour. And over time new tools and farming methods also made the farmers' lives easier, while also increasing the amount of food produced.

What do you think?

Looking at the foods from the Columbian Exchange, which ones not native to your continent are the most important to your diet? What do you think you would eat instead if they had not been spread around the world?

But for centuries, civilizations faced major **famines** (food shortages) if natural disasters affected how much grain farmers harvested. Due to limited transportation options, groups of people could not rely on bringing in food from distant areas, as nations can do today if famine strikes. Famines or any other declines in food production therefore limited or reversed population growth.

But new developments in agriculture, begun just several hundred years ago, led to the continuing population growth the world still sees today. The most important of these changes sparked what has been called the Agricultural Revolution.

The first changes came in Europe, where farmers learned that planting certain crops, such as clover, alfalfa, and peas, improved the soil. Farmers developed something called **crop rotation**. This meant that they did not plant grains in the same spot every year. Instead, they systematically rotated what was grown in each field. For example, planting clover in a field added nutrients that the grains could use when they were replanted there the next year. Crop rotation kept land in the best possible condition to be used again and again.

Mechanized farming

In 18th-century England, new **mechanized** farm equipment started to appear. A horse pulling a newly designed plow could remove weeds from between rows of crops. The seed drill was another time-saving device, as it planted seeds in rows without wasting any of them.

Farm mechanization continued quickly in the 19th century. A machine known as the **thresher** separated the edible seeds from the rest of the plant. Another important machine was the **reaper**, which cut ripe grain.

Cyrus McCormick, an American, took his reaper to England in 1851, and soon it was used across the European continent.

Over the decades, reapers were used to do even more, automatically raking the cut grain and then tying it into large bundles called bales. Each improvement meant farmers had to pay fewer people to help them raise their crops. They could plant more grain and harvest it faster.

In the United States, which was still being settled during this period, there was an abundance of cheap land, but a shortage of workers. This made the use of machines essential in U.S. farming. Farmers increasingly relied on machines to do more of the work.

JETHRO TULL

English farmer Jethro Tull (1674–1741) was trained as a lawyer, but in 1701 he designed a workable seed drill (pictured below) that improved the planting process. A horse pulled the machine, which had three hoes to dig three separate rows. Seeds then fell through a large funnel into the rows. Tull's invention was not widely used until the 19th century, as some farmers resisted changing their ways.

By the mid 1800s, farm equipment such as this seed drill was more common on British and American farms.

New immigrants also often bought their own cheap farmland, rather than work for someone else.

As machines took over many farming chores, more people were available to work in other industries. In England, many people found work in the first factories, which were built to spin thread and make cloth. In this way, the Agricultural Revolution helped make possible the Industrial Revolution, the period beginning in the late 18th century when factories and industry developed.

Increasing supplies

The Agricultural Revolution seemed to disprove the fears of some social thinkers. These thinkers had worried that the human population would consistently rise faster than the food supply, and that this would create huge social and economic problems. Improved farm technology offered hope, however, as machines allowed for more crops to be produced than ever before.

Starting with the 18th-century changes in agriculture, a growing number of people left **rural** areas, where farming had been the main source of jobs and income. They flocked to cities of all sizes, looking for work. That movement has continued over the centuries. In 1900, only 13 percent of the world's population lived in urban (city) areas. Today, just over half of the world's population does. Modern agricultural methods let fewer people produce more food for more **consumers**.

The Last 100 Years

Try to picture rural life in 1900. If you look out over the English countryside or the hills of New England in the United States, you see horses or mules pulling the farm machines invented during the previous decades. The farms are typically small and might raise several different crops.

Skip ahead 99 years, to the end of the 20th century. Across the West, the number of farms and farmworkers has fallen dramatically. In the United States, about 40 percent of all employees worked on farms in 1900. A century later, less than 2 percent did. And using farm animals for power was a thing of the past. Mechanized farming now means using tractors or self-propelled threshers and reapers. These machines often roll over huge farms that produce just a single crop—perhaps wheat, soybeans, or corn.

This change toward modern farming did not happen everywhere at the same pace. Even today, in some parts of the world, animal power helps to plant and harvest crops. But the agricultural changes of the 20th century set in motion today's most common agricultural practices, which produce food for a worldwide market.

Increasing production

One of these changes was the introduction of new **fertilizers**. Natural fertilizers, such as **manure**, had been used for thousands of years.

In some parts of the world, animals, not machines, still help farmers raise their crops.

During the 1800s, scientists identified several key chemicals that improved crop health and boosted their production. German chemist Justus von Liebig showed that the three major chemicals in soil are nitrogen, phosphorous, and potassium. If soil lacks any one of these, the crops will suffer.

Based on that knowledge, 20th-century scientists looked for new sources of these chemicals. Ammonia, for example, could be **synthesized** (artificially created) out of nitrogen in the air, and then turned into a form of nitrogen that could be used as a fertilizer. Other chemical nutrients were synthesized from petroleum. The new synthetic chemicals allowed grains and vegetables to be grown almost anywhere, rather than just on ideal soil. That in turn increased how much farmers could grow.

Rothamsted Research

Rothamsted, England, is home to the oldest site for the study of agricultural science. In 1843 two scientists there began studying the impact of fertilizers on various crops.

Some of the studies begun in Rothamsted during the 19th century continue today. One of these focuses on wheat. Scientists have compared the **yield** of fields fertilized with different combinations of chemical fertilizers—and some with no fertilizers at all.

Since the 1950s, scientists at Rothamsted Research have researched how different chemicals affect crop yields. They have also increased knowledge of the small **organisms** (living creatures) that live in the soil and help or hurt certain crops.

Reaching more consumers

Another major change in food production was the ability to transport food over long distances. Several developments led to this:

The canning process: This kept many fruits and vegetables from spoiling. Canning had been invented in the 19th century, but the mass production of canned goods, helped by large machines in factories, soared during the 20th century.

Improved transportation: This meant that food spent less time traveling from the farm to the table.

Refrigerating and freezing foods: This meant foods could stay fresh as they traveled.

These changes meant that people in many places, including cities, could eat a wider variety of crops all year round. The food did not have to come from local farms. The changes also lowered the prices for many foods.

Knowing they had a worldwide market, farmers expanded their farms. Farmers often grew one crop that could be shipped anywhere. They also focused on **economy of scale**. This is the idea that doing one thing on a large scale helps lower overall costs. For example, farmers do not need to spend much more money to plant and harvest 40 or 400 hectares (100 or 1,000 acres) of wheat than they do to plant just 4 hectares (10 acres). The basic expenses for equipment and supplies are similar in either case. As overall production rises, the cost to produce each bushel of grain falls. Then, even if prices for the crop remain the same, farmers can make more money because of the volume they have to sell.

But, over time, even producing more of a crop did not guarantee a good income. Producing more of something tends to lower the price in the market. This reflects the notion of **supply and demand**. When demand for a product is high, its cost will rise if the supply is low. When the supply is high and demand is flat or falling, the price lowers.

Lower prices meant farmers paid their workers less. Over the course of the 20th century, rural farmworkers became some of the world's worst-paid workers, especially in countries without a lot of mechanized farming. In the Philippines, for example, figures from 1988 showed that almost half of the country's rural farmworkers lived in poverty. In wealthy countries, such as the United States, few people wanted to do hard farmwork for low pay. Many regions relied on migrants, who are immigrants who travel from region to region as different crops are harvested.

Limits to progress: Famine

Despite all the agricultural advances brought about by improved machinery and fertilizers, famines still occurred. During the 1930s, for example, a huge famine struck the Soviet Union. Politics played a part, as Soviet leader Joseph Stalin took grain grown in what is now the nation of Ukraine and sold it overseas. He wanted the money to build up his country's industry. But nature also had a hand in this disaster. For several seasons, first too much rain fell, then too little. The farmers had already sent most of their grain to the cities. They did not have enough left in reserve when the bad weather struck. Several million people died during the famine. The Ukraine famine and more recent ones show that human actions and nature together can upset the balance of food production.

The mass production of canned foods was a major factor in changing the world's food economy.

Later breakthroughs

By the mid-20th century, science and technology were more important than ever in the world. In Western nations, in particular, people increasingly believed that science and technology could solve almost any problem. For example, new drugs had appeared, such as penicillin, that could treat many diseases. Science and technology also played a big role in agriculture.

Synthetic fertilizers had already proven the value of chemicals. Scientists—especially at Rothamsted Research (see page 13)—then began to introduce **herbicides** and **pesticides**.

One of these pesticides was DDT. It killed many different insects without seeming to harm other animals that came into a treated field. The chemical was also not easily washed away by rains. DDT helped further increase the production of farms around the world.

Scientists also looked to create better seeds and farming methods, as part of what became known as the Green Revolution. This revolution involved greatly increasing grain production through using improved kinds of seeds and farming methods.

Fast-growing strains of rice were introduced in India. In Mexico, farmers grew shorter strains of corn. These plants put their energy into creating more seeds, rather than tall stalks.

In dry climates, scientist looked for ways to grow crops with as little water as possible. Some of the best work took place in Israel, which has hot, dry summers. Symcha Blass, originally from Great Britain, settled in Israel and developed a form of drip **irrigation**. Long plastic tubes carried water to the plants and released it in small drips directly on the roots. Israeli drip irrigation is now used around the world, and Israel's farms are so productive that they send large amounts of citrus fruits to Europe.

Some regions lack both water and suitable land for growing crops. One solution is hydroponics—growing the plants directly in liquids filled with nutrients. People have known about hydroponics for thousands of years, but 20th-century researchers specifically studied how to use hydroponics to grow food crops.

Hydroponic farming takes place indoors and can be more expensive than field-based agriculture. But it allows for growing vegetables year-round in places where crops will not grow outside. And the crops are often larger and healthier than similar ones grown in soil. Some scientists say hydroponics could one day be used to grow crops for astronauts on long space missions.

This lettuce grows using a mixture of water and chemicals instead of soil, a method called hydroponics.

NORMAN BORLAUG

The "Green Revolution" refers to the rapid increase in the production of grains in **developing countries** during the later decades of the 20th century. Scientists from Western nations led this effort. One man is most often associated with this process: U.S. scientist Norman Borlaug (1914–2009).

In some of his earliest work, Borlaug led the effort to develop and plant wheat that would resist disease and produce more food. Then he focused on India. Starvation was common there after World War II (1939–45) ended. Borlaug helped the Indians plant new strains of rice that increased production. The country had rice shortages before the Green Revolution. Afterward, it had enough extra rice to sell to other countries. Some experts estimated that Borlaug's efforts with the Green Revolution saved the lives of hundreds of millions of people in India and other parts of the world. Use the chart below to see how India's food system and population have changed since 1950:

	1950	1960	1970	1980	1990	2000
Food grain production (metric tons)	50.8	82	108.4	129.6	176.4	201.8
Food grain imports (metric tons)	4.6	10.4	7.5	.8	.3	--
Population (millions)	361	439	548	683	846	1,000

"You can't build a peaceful world on empty stomachs and human misery."
—Norman Borlaug

Unwanted Consequences

The progression of farming, from raising the first domesticated plants to modern agriculture, has created great food abundance. The increase in production of grains and other crops has fueled the world's rapid population growth over the last few centuries. In 1900 the world population was 1.65 billion. By 2000 it had leaped to 6.06 billion.

But along with the abundance have come several unwanted results, mostly affecting the environment and human health. If current farming practices remain in place, these problems could continue to grow. Scientists and other people are trying to find ways to eliminate the problems, while keeping agricultural production high.

What do you think?

While the use of chemicals causes environmental problems, it does help feed more people. Thanks to mechanized farming and the use of chemicals, there has been a dramatic increase in available food throughout the world. An international group that promotes ending famine said, "No country has been able to expand agricultural growth rates and eliminate hunger without increasing fertilizer use." What do you think? Is the damage to the environment worth it if chemical fertilizers help feed more people? Or are there solutions that can balance saving the environment with feeding many people?

A chemical stew

No one denies that pesticides, herbicides, and synthetic fertilizers have helped farmers grow more grain and other crops. From 1965 to 2007, world grain production more than doubled, from .823 billion tonnes (.91 billion tons) to 1.9 billion tonnes (2.1 billion tons).

But as early as the 1960s, some scientists wondered about the effects of agricultural chemicals on the environment. Rachel Carson was one of the first to sound the alarm, with her book *Silent Spring*. She was concerned about the possible dangers of the pesticide DDT.

RACHEL CARSON

Something was killing the birds—and the evidence clearly showed that the pesticide DDT was the cause. In 1957 the state of Massachusetts used DDT to control mosquitoes, but farmers also used it to kill insects threatening their crops. Scientist Rachel Carson (1907–1964) heard about the dead birds and began to investigate. She published her findings in the 1962 book *Silent Spring.* Carson warned that DDT and other powerful chemicals were a threat to humans, animals, and the entire Earth.

Silent Spring sparked a heated debate. Carson's critics said that she was ignoring the benefits of pesticides, which were so useful in agriculture. Carson said she did not want to get rid of all of them—just the most dangerous ones, like DDT. She also thought other pesticides should be used less often, and that scientists should look for safer ways to control damaging insects. Thanks to *Silent Spring*, DDT was eventually banned in many countries. Some countries, though, still use it to kill mosquitoes that carry diseases such as malaria.

Carson is considered the founder of modern **environmentalism**. Her work led the United States to pass its first laws addressing water and air pollution. It also made other scientists consider the possible long-term effects of synthetic chemicals on the environment.

Rachel Carson first won fame for writing several books about the world's oceans.

Today, billions of tons of pesticides are still used by farmers around the world. But, in response to some scientists' concerns that widespread pesticide use can harm the environment, some farmers have come to rely on them less in recent years. Part of the reduction comes from **organic** farmers, who choose not to use any chemicals to grow their crops (see pages 46 and 47). New kinds of pesticides have also helped the problem. Farmers need to apply smaller amounts of these pesticides to effectively kill harmful insects. The new pesticides are also less toxic to humans and the environment as a whole.

Problems remain, however, with disposing of old agricultural chemicals. In some poor countries, old or unused pesticides are stored in barrels. Some of these pesticides have been banned because new research has shown they are too dangerous to use. Farmers or government agencies simply leave the barrels in old warehouses or in crude shelters because they lack the money to safely store or get rid of the chemicals. Over time, these pesticides can sometimes leak out and enter the soil or local water supplies.

A 2009 study in Tunisia showed that the African nation had almost 1,800 tonnes (2,000 tons) of pesticides at sites where they were leaking. Pesticides at several of the sites threatened to enter lakes and kill fish. In response, the Tunisian government began working on a plan to clean up the worst of the storage sites.

Old barrels of pesticide are placed in special containers to prevent the chemicals from leaking.

Fertilizers: Growth versus nutrients

The use of fertilizers has also been shown to create problems with the nutritional content of crops. While the use of fertilizers causes grains to grow quickly, it may also cause the grains to be robbed of some minerals found deep in the soil. A 2007 report cited data from both the United States and the United Kingdom. It showed that many crops had lower amounts of several important minerals called micronutrients—such as zinc, iron, and selenium—than they had had in the past. People need small amounts of these micronutrients to stay healthy.

What causes this problem? Crops grown with chemical fertilizers do not have to grow deep roots to get their main nutrients of nitrogen, phosphorous, and potassium. They put most of their energy into growing larger seeds or fruit, rather than extending their roots into the soil. The shallow roots mean the crops also do not take in the naturally occurring micronutrients deeper in the soil. The ultimate result is that the food people prepare from these crops also lacks the micronutrients, most of which are important for human health.

Health watch

Selenium

The decline of micronutrients in the soil has stirred a debate. U.S. government information from 2009 says most people around the world still received enough of the micronutrient selenium from the food they eat. But how much is enough? On the one hand, low levels of selenium have been linked to higher risk of certain diseases, such as heart disease. On the other hand, some studies suggest that amounts of selenium much higher than what people can get from grains and meat may help fight cancer or other diseases. According to these studies, people should be getting even more selenium and other micronutrients than they currently do. But these claims have not been proven, and scientists are not sure just how much selenium people need.

Fertilizers have caused other problems in the relationship between crops and soil minerals. Organisms called fungi live underground. (The mushrooms you may enjoy in salads or spaghetti sauce are one kind of fungi.) Some fungi grow on the roots of crops, which have sugar that the fungi use as a source of food. These kinds of fungi are called mycorrhizae, from the Latin word for "fungus" and the Greek word for "root." Mycorrhizae appear on more than 90 percent of all the world's plants. Mycorrhizae perform a variety of services to agricultural crops, including providing them with soil minerals.

An Indian farmer displays dry crops. The use of synthetic fertilizers in India since the 1960s has helped lead to modern water shortages.

But long-term use of chemical fertilizers and pesticides has been shown to reduce the mycorrhizae in the soil. To solve this problem, some companies now sell natural fertilizers with mycorrhizae in them, to help return the fungi to the soil. Tests have shown that using these fertilizers helps restore valuable nutrients to the crops. This approach does not fully solve the problem, but it is an effective partial solution.

Environment watch

Revolt against the Green Revolution

The proof is clear—India's Green Revolution of the 1960s (see page 17) saved lives. People who otherwise would have starved had enough to eat. But in recent years, some Indians and international experts have questioned the long-term effects of that revolution.

Following the direction of Western scientists, Indians began irrigating their fields and using synthetic fertilizers. The seeds they used grew quickly, but these seeds required more water than the local crops farmers once grew. Farmers had to dig wells to get the extra water.

Today, some parts of India face water shortages, and a few farmers must dig down 60 meters (200 feet) to find underground wells. Digging and then pumping the water costs money, meaning the farmers make less from their farms. And some of the water they tap contains salt, which kills the crops. In general, the Indian farmers also use more fertilizer than they used to, since the soil has lost nutrients. This also adds to their expenses. At times, the farmers have to borrow money to run their farms, but they do not make enough to pay back what they owe.

The long-term problems of the Green Revolution have led some Indians to return to traditional farming methods. But the country's population is still growing, and so the demand for food is rising. The methods of the Green Revolution might be the only ones that can provide the food—but at a cost to some Indian farmers.

What do you think?

Do the benefits of the Green Revolution outweigh the problems it has caused? Why or why not?

Dead zones

One problem with agricultural chemicals is that they do not always stay where they are used. Rain and irrigation water can carry the chemicals off the fields and into rivers and streams. In particular, nitrogen is found in 60 percent of the fertilizer used to grow cereal crops. Rain carries this nitrogen into rivers, which then carry it into oceans and seas.

"The biggest contributor of nitrogen to marine systems is agriculture. It's the same scenario all over the world. Farmers are not doing it on purpose. They'd prefer to have it stick on the land."
—Scientist Robert Diaz

This nitrogen plays a huge role in many outbreaks of something called hypoxia, which is the lack of enough oxygen in water to support sea life. Nitrogen is food for tiny sea life called algae. With a larger food supply, an algae population can explode—more food makes it easier for more algae to live and then reproduce. Eventually, though, the increased algae population dies as part of its natural life cycle. It then becomes food for even smaller organisms, which use up oxygen in the water as they eat their algae meals. The resulting lack of oxygen kills any sea life that cannot easily leave the area for healthier waters.

Nitrogen and global warming

Nitrogen from fertilizers also plays a role in **global warming**, the gradual increase in temperatures across Earth. Organisms in fertilized soil eat some of the nitrogen and create nitrous oxide in the process. Nitrous oxide is one of the so-called **greenhouse gases** that rise above Earth and trap heat in the atmosphere. These gases and the trapping of heat are thought to be part of the reason for global warming. In the U.S., the government estimates that two-thirds of the nitrous oxide the country produces comes from farming.

When hypoxia becomes severe, it can kill thousands of tons of fish that humans normally catch for food. Scientists have identified several hundred "dead zones" around the world, meaning areas in the world's oceans and seas that lack enough oxygen to support sea life—and the number is rising.

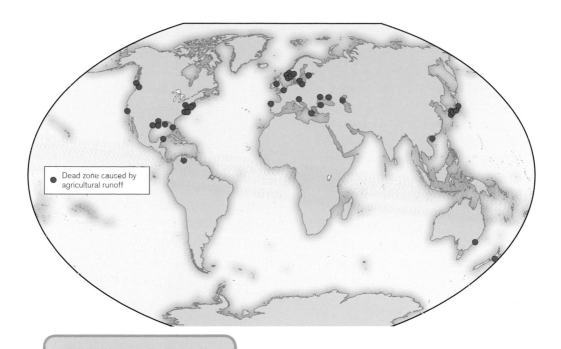

In 2011, the world had more than 500 dead zones. This map shows the locations of some of the worst.

Scientists are exploring several ways to reduce the amount of nitrogen farms use, which means less will run off into the world's bodies of water. One method has already been successfully used—breeding crops that use nitrogen more efficiently. The more of the chemical the crops actually absorb, the less is leftover to create a harmful runoff.

Some types of wheat now use 20 to 40 percent more of the available nitrogen than older types did.

The other major focus is on changing the genes of crops so they will use nitrogen more efficiently. Some tests have shown that crops modified this way can produce the same yield with half as much fertilizer as farmers normally use. But the idea of **genetic engineering** in agriculture remains controversial.

Clearing forests and fields

Nitrogen is not the only farming factor that affects global warming. In parts of the world, farmers clear forests so they can raise more crops. In recent decades, much of this activity has taken place in the world's rain forests. These and other forests are vital to the world's health. Trees consume the gas carbon dioxide, which is one of the major greenhouse gases. The trees then release oxygen. Rain forests are also home to much of the planet's wildlife. South America's Amazon Rain Forest, which covers 8,235,430 square kilometers (3,179,715 square miles), has 30 percent of the world's plant and animal species.

The destruction of rain forests for agriculture and other uses has been rising in the Amazon and elsewhere. Part of the reason is that major agricultural companies want to raise a single crop for distant markets (see page 35). These include soy, cacao, and coffee.

Agriculture and global warming

Farming itself is a major contributor to the problem of global warming. Livestock, particularly cattle, release methane, one of the greenhouse gases. And transporting food over long distances usually requires the burning of fossil fuels, which also creates harmful gases.

Many scientists fear that global warming could damage agriculture in many ways. The melting of polar ice could cause ocean waters to rise, flooding low-lying areas. Changing weather patterns could also limit the growing of crops in areas that are now especially fertile.

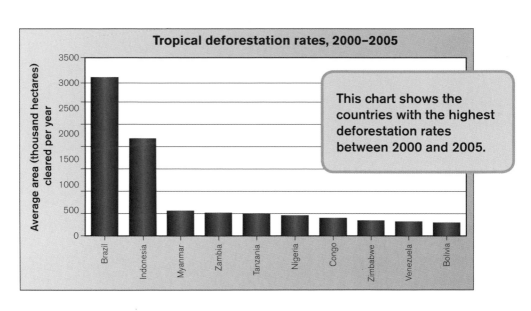

Tropical deforestation rates, 2000–2005

Average area (thousand hectares) cleared per year

Brazil, Indonesia, Myanmar, Zambia, Tanzania, Nigeria, Congo, Zimbabwe, Venezuela, Bolivia

This chart shows the countries with the highest deforestation rates between 2000 and 2005.

Another factor is the movement of local people into new parts of the forests. Large-scale farming or logging pushes these people off their traditional lands. They seek new lands, where they carry out "slash-and-burn" farming—a method sometimes used by the first farmers thousands of years ago. The local residents clear out a small area of farmland, cutting and burning the existing plant life. After a few years, the soil loses its nutrients, and then the people move on, repeating the cycle.

The spread of agriculture into the rain forests leads to other problems as well. The plants in a rain forest can affect the climate in nearby regions. The trees and other plants slowly release water into the air. This moisture then returns to Earth as rainfall. As trees are cut, the rain forests release less moisture, which can reduce rainfall amounts even beyond the forests. In recent years, **droughts** have occurred in the Amazon and the rain forests of Southeast Asia.

The loss of trees, in rain forests and elsewhere, can also cause problems on the ground. The roots of trees and other plants help keep soil in place during heavy rains. Without the trees, the soil is carried away into nearby rivers—a process called erosion. The soil that remains behind is less productive. Less soil also leads to flooding in some areas, since the soil on top would otherwise help absorb water. Erosion also carries agricultural chemicals into rivers and bays, possibly harming wildlife. As farmland is lost to erosion, farmers clear even more trees, looking for new places to raise their crops. The farmers need to make money, but the environment pays a price.

Large sections of the Amazon are being cleared so the land can be used to grow soybeans and raise cattle.

Case study:
Land and jobs in Indonesia

A conflict between providing jobs and protecting the environment has been going on for several years in Indonesia. For many people around the world, the fruit of the oil palm tree is an important crop. The fruit and its seed produce two types of palm oil, which is used in cooking and to make a wide range of products, including soaps. The oil can also be used for biofuel—plant-based fuels for vehicles.

The demand for palm oil is on the rise, helping to create jobs in rural areas of Indonesia, one of the top producers of the oil. But to grow more oil palm trees, farmers have cut down a lot of the country's rain forests.

One of the largest producers of the oil is the U.S. company Cargill (see box at right). For several years, it has battled environmental groups that claim its oil-palm plantations (large farms) harm the environment. Cargill says it follows international guidelines for growing the trees **sustainably**, meaning the rain forests are not damaged.

In 2010 the Rainforest Action Network claimed Cargill secretly ran two plantations that did not follow the guidelines, resulting in the destruction of more rain forest. Cargill denied the charge and announced it would work with another environmental group to make sure it followed all the agreements it had made for producing palm oil sustainably. The incident showed the conflicts that sometimes can arise as farmers try to fill a food need, while environmentalists try to protect nature.

These workers are harvesting oil palm fruit on an Indonesian plantation.

Cargill

In 1865 Cargill was founded as a grain storage company in the U.S. Midwest. Today, it has more than 130,000 workers in dozens of countries. In 2010 the company had sales of more than $107 billion and was a world leader in processing grains and livestock. Like all big businesses, Cargill's main goal is to make profits for its owners. Companies constantly look for ways to boost sales and lower their costs, in order to increase their profits. Cargill says it follows local laws and international agreements as it expands its operations in and near the world's rain forests.

But the issue in Indonesia was not the first time the company was accused of harming the environment. Cargill was also accused of playing a major role in destroying part of Brazil's rain forest. Cargill built a plant near the forest to process soybeans into cattle feed, spurring the destruction of the forest for farmland. Cargill also helped some farmers expand into the forest. Critics of large businesses like Cargill accuse them of ignoring laws or winning support from local leaders who will help them expand their business. But the companies say they help boost the local economy in poor, rural areas of the world.

What do you think?

What could Western consumers who dislike a company's practices do to try to stop its actions? Would it be more effective for consumers to talk to their local leaders, or to stop buying products from the large business?

Business, Government, and Agriculture

Across the globe, individual farmers and field workers plant, grow, and harvest the grains and other crops you eat. But thousands of miles from the farms, in government buildings and business offices, other people influence what is grown and what you eat.

Whenever farmers sell crops they do not need for themselves, they are in business. They might decide to plant more of a popular crop one year, hoping they can make more money. Seeds, equipment, chemicals, and companies are also needed for agriculture, so people create companies to fill those needs.

These are all examples of **agribusinesses**, meaning companies that make their money in areas relating to farming and food production. The name "agribusiness," though, is usually associated with the large international companies that dominate the field. And in most countries, agribusinesses work hard to shape government agricultural policies. They seek to make the most money for themselves that they can—as most businesses do.

Government policies

Governments also play a huge role in agriculture. They want to make sure their local farmers receive a good price for their grains and other crops. Falling crop prices can drive farmers out of business and increase poverty levels in rural areas, so governments do all they can to avoid this. They can take several steps to influence what farmers grow and how much money they make.

In the late 19th century, grain prices fell across Western Europe. This was because grain was reaching the continent from other areas, an increase in supply that drove prices down—a result of supply and demand. Several governments responded by placing tariffs, a kind of tax, on crops brought in from other countries. The tariffs raised the price of the foreign food and made citizens more likely to buy the local crops.

Grapes, such as these in France, are just one of the many crops that modern governments pay farmers to grow.

The Great Depression

Several decades later, in 1929 the Great Depression struck the world's economy. People lost their jobs and sometimes their homes. Even before the Depression began, farmers had seen their prices falling. In the United States, in particular, farmers had raised even more crops, hoping that by selling more they could make up for the lower price of each bushel of wheat or corn. But the demand did not rise, the grains went unsold, and prices fell further.

In the United States and other countries, governments once again stepped in. Some farmers received money not to grow certain crops. Again, supply and demand was at play. If the farmers produced less, the supply would fall, and prices would rise for the farmers still growing and selling the crop. The United Kingdom, which had not previously used tariffs to help farmers, now also saw the need to influence farmers' actions through government policies.

The growth of subsidies

After the Great Depression ended, most Western nations used **subsidies**—money paid by the government directly to farmers to influence their actions. The idea was that a government could give their farmers a boost in the world market. In 1947 the United Kingdom paid subsidies to help farmers buy fertilizer and receive credit so that they could expand their farms. In this case, the government was more interested in increasing overall production of crops, so that the British would not have to buy their food overseas.

Today, most subsidies are given to encourage farmers to grow particular crops. In Europe, members of the European Union (EU), a partnership among 27 nations, have a Common Agricultural Policy (CAP) that gives subsidies to member nations.

The United States exports (sends away) more food than any other country, with sales of food, feed, and beverage of more than $100 billion a year. Since the end of World War II, its subsidies to farmers have risen, and they now total between $20 billion and $30 billion every year. The subsidies mostly target the production of wheat, corn, soybean, and dairy products.

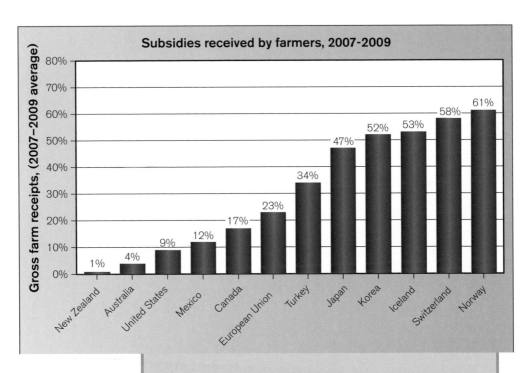

This chart shows the percentage of money farmers received from government subsidies in select countries, 2007-2009.

Results of subsidies

Since farmers receive money to grow these crops, they tend to raise as much as they can. Many of the subsidized crops are then sold at low prices around the world. Consumers in distant lands benefit, since they can pay less for flour or bread. This can also make the meat the United States buys from overseas cheaper, since the animals there were fed on subsidized corn.

But there is a downside. Farmers overseas cannot compete with subsidized crops from the United States or other Western nations. And farmworkers in those countries receive wages so low that they often live in poverty.

Subsidies are not given equally to all farmers. In the United Kingdom, the EU, and the United States, a small percentage of farmers receive most of the subsidies. Some of the money goes to wealthy people who own farmland and rent it to the actual farmers. The owners get the money, even though they do not directly farm the land.

Subsidies and livestock

Subsidies usually do not go to the farmers who raise the most fruits and vegetables, foods that scientists know have many health benefits. The subsidies, instead, go primarily to growers of corn and other grains that are also used to feed livestock. Often the foods made from these crops are not healthy (see pages 38 and 39). Cheap corn and grains are also used to fatten cattle and pigs, which become a cheap source of animal protein for consumers. Dairy cows and chicken produce milk and eggs. The abundance of grain leads to lower prices for all those products.

Health watch

Grass-fed livestock

Most livestock are fed cheap grains. But it has been shown that most livestock are healthier—and produce healthier products—when they are fed grass. Humans eat less of several key nutrients when they eat products from animals fed grain instead of grass.

In the United States, some sources say, almost all cattle are fed corn during most of their lives. Pure pasture-raised (grass-fed) beef still represents less than 1 percent of the nation's supply. But sales reached some $120 million last year and are expected to increase more than 20 percent a year over the next decade, reflecting an increased awareness of this issue.

Food safety

In the worldwide food system, governments do more than provide subsidies and open new markets overseas. For decades, they have also played a role in watching over agriculture, to make sure food production is safe—from the farm, to the factory, to the table. In the United States, the Department of Agriculture (USDA) oversees the growing of crops and the raising of livestock. The Food and Drug Administration (FDA) watches over food ingredients for safety, among other missions.

A "revolving door"?

While food safety agencies play an important role in the food system, they sometimes face criticism. Some government workers in the food agencies once worked for agribusiness or promoted their interests to U.S. lawmakers. Critics talk about a "revolving door" that sends these people to a string of jobs in industry and government. Some people fear that agribusiness can use this door to influence government food policies. Its former workers serving in government agencies may be tempted to promote the interests of agribusiness over the public good, or may at least be more sympathetic to the companies.

This microbiologist is preparing to test a lettuce sample for dangerous organisms such as salmonella.

> "To forget how to dig the earth and to tend the
> soil is to forget ourselves."
> —Indian leader Mahatma Gandhi

These and similar government agencies act when a health hazard enters the food supply. In recent years, salmonella has appeared on different crops sold in markets, such as black pepper, peanuts, and hot peppers. Salmonella is a tiny organism that can make people sick or, in extreme cases, kill them. The government agencies provide information so that consumers can identify foods that might have a problem and get rid of them before they eat them.

"Superfarms"

Modern agribusinesses began to develop about 70 years ago. The United States, with its huge agricultural output, took the lead. In 1956 one U.S. official told farmers they would have to "get big or get out" to meet the needs of the largest food processors. Today, about half of U.S. farms are less than 40 hectares (99 acres). But the average is more than 160 hectares (400 acres), and some "superfarms" cover more than 800 hectares (2,000 acres)—an area the size of some small towns, or 2,000 soccer fields.

Monoculture

Farmers growing for agribusinesses tend to focus on one crop, a practice called monoculture. ("Mono" comes from the Greek word for "one.") Large-scale farmers focus on crops, usually grains, that produce high yields with the lowest expense, and the ones most in demand by the food processors. These are also crops that are subsidized by governments.

Monoculture, though, has some problems. Growing only one crop every year, such as corn, takes nutrients out of the soil. Crop rotation—for example, growing other grasses that return nutrients to the soil—is one solution. But crops such as grasses do not make money for a farmer, so most farmers do not choose this option. Instead, large monoculture farms simply add more chemical nutrients, so that they can keep growing their money-making crop.

Another issue with monoculture is plant disease. If a disease that affects a monoculture crop, such as wheat, hits a farm where only wheat is grown, the farmer could lose an entire year's crop—and income. Monoculture also limits biodiversity—the idea that having as many plants and animals as possible is good for the overall environment.

The struggle to compete with agribusiness

Agribusiness practices have created personal problems for some of the world's small farmers. The huge supply of grains created by agribusiness helps keep the cost of the grains low. But some farmers with small operations do not have the same economy of scale as the large companies and have trouble competing. An agribusiness, for example, might be able to sell rice for a cheaper price than what it costs an Indian farmer to grow it. As a result, in India and other parts of the world, farmers have struggled to compete with agribusiness, and some fall into poverty.

The push for cheap food also often means lower wages for many farmworkers. Many give up on farmwork and head to cities, hoping to find new jobs. Others might leave their country altogether and seek work on farms in other lands. For several years, hundreds of thousands of Nicaraguans have traveled to other parts of Central America, looking for farmwork they could not find at home.

Industrialized farming

Agribusinesses have led the way in what some food experts called **industrialized farming**. More than using huge machines to harvest and process food, this kind of farming also relies on scientific knowledge. Some of the knowledge leads to more effective pesticides and herbicides. Other scientific efforts focus on producing new strains of crops that will naturally resist pests or grow faster.

The size of the largest agribusinesses gives them great power. Monsanto, for example, is a world leader in selling seeds to farmers. It uses genetic engineering (see pages 42 and 43) to create seeds for many crops. The plants grown from the seeds have a special trait—they will not die when sprayed with the herbicide called Roundup, which Monsanto also makes.

Only Monsanto produces these "Roundup Ready" crops, so farmers who want them have to pay whatever price Monsanto asks. They also have to follow the rules Monsanto sets down for growing their genetically engineered plants (see the box at right).

Monsanto says farmers benefit because Roundup Ready and other engineered plants require less care in the field. It gives the farmers more time for themselves and to be with their families. But critics say the higher cost of Monsanto seeds and the company's tight control over how they are used can create financial hardship for some farmers.

This researcher is working with genetically engineered soybean plants in a Monsanto greenhouse facility.

Plant ownership?

Monsanto does not let farmers use the seeds from Roundup Ready crops to raise a new year's crop. It claims that the genetic changes it made to the plant means the company owns the plant. The farmers are only paying for the right to grow one year's yield. They must buy new seeds for the crop the next year. Monsanto enforces this policy strictly, sending workers out to investigate and make sure farmers are not using Roundup Ready crops without its permission.

The Canadian Supreme Court said Monsanto can legally claim that it owns the seeds it modifies. Monsanto can require farmers to pay for the use of Roundup Ready seeds every year. Several members of the court, however, believed Monsanto and other companies could not claim ownership of the seeds produced by a plant grown from one of their modified seeds.

Industrialized processing

While agribusinesses like Monsanto focus on seeds, other agribusiness companies focus on processing grains and other crops into food.

In a typical supermarket, you might see thousands of items. But many of them contain different forms of just a few crops, along with meat or dairy. Soy, corn, sugar, and wheat are major subsidized crops that turn up in many foods. In many cases, these subsidized crops are changed into new substances that can be used in cheap, processed foods, such as fast foods. Wheat, for example, is often milled into white, or refined, flour. The refining process removes parts of the grain with the most nutrients, however, making these crops less healthy.

Crackers are just one of the grain-based foods that are processed using machinery.

Corn is often turned into a sweetener called high-fructose corn syrup. The syrup itself may or may not be harmful; scientists are not sure. But it is often used in foods that are high in calories and low in nutrients, such as sweetened drinks and processed snacks. For the average American, more than half of the sweeteners in the foods they eat come from corn. Outside the United States, nations that do not grow much corn are likely to import processed foods that contain corn or high-fructose corn syrup. Foods high in sugar—and fat—are thought to lead to obesity (being severely overweight), which in turn can create other health problems.

Non-food products

Subsidized crops also turn up in non-food products. Both corn and soybeans are used for fuels, as nations try to use less petroleum. Processed corn products also turn up in some medical and health products, such as vitamins. And some corn is turned into a form of plastic used to package other foods.

But some people question the use of crops for fuel and other products, when some people around the world are going hungry. The use of crops as fuels could also raise the overall cost of corn and other important crops.

Sugar, fat, and salt

Many processed foods have sugar, fat, and salt in them for a reason: humans are, by nature, drawn to these tastes. But in the early days of hunter-gatherers, people did not find huge amounts of foods with these substances. Now, though, processed foods often provide large amounts of sugar, fat, and salt—more than is healthy. The foods high in them, such as a meal at a fast-food restaurant, provide lots of calories at a cheap price. But the calories are not as nutritious as those in fruits or vegetables, which are typically low in fat, sugar, and salt. But fast-food calories are often cheaper than fresh produce, which is why some people choose them.

What do you think?

Would you give up certain foods you like if you found out they were not good for you because they contained sugar or fat? What if those foods were also cheaper than other foods that you like that were better for you? What if you had a family to feed and did not have a lot of money to spend on food?

The Future of Food

Imagine it is 2050—slightly over nine billion people now live across the planet. Is there enough food for everyone? Can everyone afford it?

In 2010 the Food and Agriculture Organization of the United Nations (FAO), along with another international group, predicted that the world would need to produce 70 percent more food to feed everyone in 2050. Most of the growth in demand will come in developing countries, which today are not as wealthy as the Western nations.

The populations of these developing nations will grow, and so will their wealth. As in China in recent decades, people will look to buy more expensive foods, such as meat. More grains will be needed to feed the livestock used for meat. And the sheer rise in population will mean production of all kinds of crops will have to increase. Increasingly, developing countries will produce more of their own food, as China and India have been doing.

The FAO believes the world's farmers will be able to grow enough food for everyone. **Food security** will continue to be a major problem, though. This is the idea that all people should have easy access to affordable, nutritious food. Can governments get all the food to the people who need it? And will the food provide for everyone's nutritional needs?

The future of agricultural production

The 2010 FAO report made detailed predictions for agricultural production through 2019. The following are some of its estimates for the increase in production of certain crops, over the amount produced in 2007–2008:

Crop	Estimated increase
Wheat	14%
Rice	15%
Sugar	23%
Vegetable oils	39%

Before a 2009 meeting on food security in Rome, many protesters gathered to call for policies that would end hunger.

"Our job is not just to feed the hungry, but to empower the hungry to feed themselves."
—Ban Ki-moon, secretary general of the United Nations

The issue is really one of poverty. Countries need to find ways for all their citizens to make enough money to buy healthy food. Except in times of war or famine, enough food is usually available for everyone, if they can afford it.

UN officials believe another key issue for the future of food is having countries cooperate. They need to pursue food policies that help everyone, and not just one nation's farmers. In 2009 UN Secretary General Ban Ki-moon called for an end to subsidizing crops and to laws that make it hard for small farmers to sell their goods in foreign nations. The wealthy Western nations, however, have been slow to reduce their major farm subsidies.

Ban and the FAO also stress the need to address climate change, a term that refers to the general global warming of the past few decades (see pages 24 to 27). Changes in temperature and rainfall could make it hard to grow crops in some regions—though other parts of the world might be able to produce more than they do now. Scientists cannot say for sure how agriculture will change, but most agree it will change if average temperatures continue to rise.

Large food-producing companies will continue to play an important role in agriculture. Their success gives them the money to look for new ways to improve agriculture through science and technology. One of the major changes for the future has already begun—genetic engineering. By changing the genes in certain crops, scientists can produce new varieties with desirable traits.

All living organisms have genes, which contain chemicals that determine their traits. The genes are passed on from one generation to the next. In nature small changes can occur over time. But in the lab, scientists add new genetic material to create a quick and specific change to an organism's traits.

In agriculture, scientists have engineered tomatoes that stayed on the vine longer without rotting. Much of the corn grown today has been altered so that it can naturally resist harmful insects, so farmers do not have to use pesticides. And both corn and soybeans are commonly altered to withstand Monsanto's Roundup herbicide. In the future, agribusiness firms will likely perfect genetically engineered crops that can resist drought.

The fight against GMOs

Crops with altered genes are often called **genetically modified organisms (GMOs)**, or GM foods. Since the introduction of the first GMOs during the 1990s, some food groups and scientists have opposed their use. The first critics called GMOs "Frankenfood," referring to the fictional Frankenstein monster. In the story, the doctor who created the monster did not know what his monster would do. Those who oppose genetically modified foods say agribusiness does not know what these new crops might do to humans or the environment.

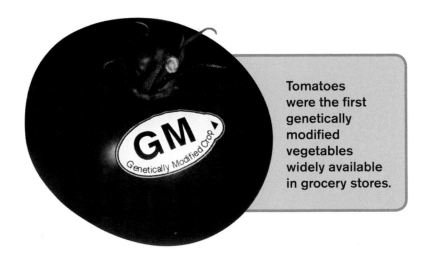

Tomatoes were the first genetically modified vegetables widely available in grocery stores.

Some environmental groups fear genes from the altered crops could get mixed with natural plants, and then no one knows what the effects might be. In 2010 scientists found genetically modified canola growing wild in part of the United States. The plants had genes from two different kinds of canola designed to resist two different kinds of pesticides. The wild canola now resisted both. The scientists feared the wild canola could become a weed that farmers could not easily kill.

Greenpeace is one of many international organizations fighting the spread of GMOs. Along with fearing possible environmental problems, it cites reports that show genetically engineered farming can sometimes be more expensive for farmers. And Roundup Ready soybeans yield less per acre than originally claimed—and less than non-altered soybeans. Yet a new version of the seed costs more than other soybean seeds. In 2010 members of Greenpeace traveled across Europe seeking support for their call to end the farming of GMOs on the continent.

However, the companies that make genetically altered crops argue that poor farmers will benefit from their product, as they plant crops that do not need as much water or chemical treatments, and that are therefore cheaper to raise.

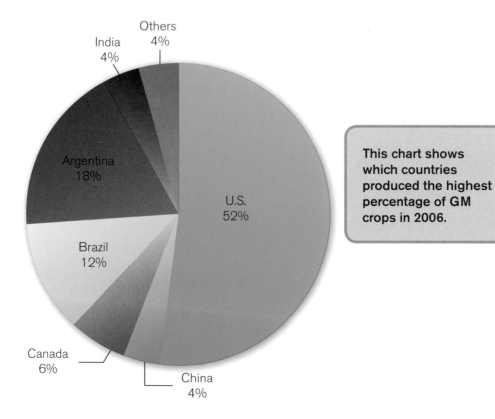

This chart shows which countries produced the highest percentage of GM crops in 2006.

International battles over GMOs

The debate over GMOs has involved international battles as well. The EU has stopped the sale of genetically modified corn grown in the United States, Canada, and several other nations. The Europeans argue that these countries have not done proper tests to see if their GMOs are safe. The United States led a legal battle to end the ban. In 2006 the World Trade Organization ruled that the EU ban was unfair and should be lifted. The Europeans, however, continued to keep genetically modified corn from abroad out of their countries.

Back to the old ways

As the debate over GMOs goes on, some farmers are looking for ways to grow crops without relying so much on chemicals and advanced science. This effort is called sustainable agriculture. The term "sustainable" means different things to different people. In general, however, farming sustainably means using methods that limit damage to the environment. In particular, sustainable agriculture tries to protect the soil, water supplies, animals, and humans, while also conserving energy and promoting recycling. It can be applied to small farms growing vegetables for a local market or farms of several thousand acres growing wheat or soybeans.

For some people, sustainable agriculture also means changing the current food system. This means limiting the power of agribusiness to influence what people eat and creating food security. As part of the sustainable food movement, some people call for taking more time to enjoy meals. Followers of the "slow food" movement say that people should try to avoid fast food restaurants, get to know their local farmers, and truly savor the most nutritious food possible.

Labeling

Many people argue that foods containing genetically altered ingredients should be clearly labeled. In the United States, agribusiness has convinced the government to not place these labels on GM foods. They believe people have an unnecessary fear of GMOs, based on the messages of groups like Greenpeace (see page 43). The companies say scientists have shown that GMOs are safe in agriculture. Critics of the GMOs say consumers should have a right to know as much as possible about what they eat. Then they can decide for themselves whether or not to eat food with altered corn or soy. The EU requires companies to label foods that contain GMOs.

Global sustainability

The effort to grow more crops sustainably is global, and some countries are working together to achieve that goal. In 2008 China and the United Kingdom created the Sustainable Agriculture Innovation Network (SAIN). The aim was to unite a developed, Western nation with a developing country to share knowledge about new sustainable methods. The next year, eight leading industrialized nations, including the United Kingdom and the United States, said the lack of food security was one of the world's most serious issues. U.S officials saw promoting sustainable agriculture in all developing nations as one way to combat it. Sustainable farming practices would create a larger supply of local food, while helping the environment.

> "[T]he risk lies in not using biotechnology [genetic engineering] . . . in not using science to solve our problems of hunger, malnutrition, inhospitable areas where it's difficult to farm."
> —Dr. Luciana Di Ciero, Brazilian scientist

This map shows the parts of Europe where GMOs are not allowed to be grown.

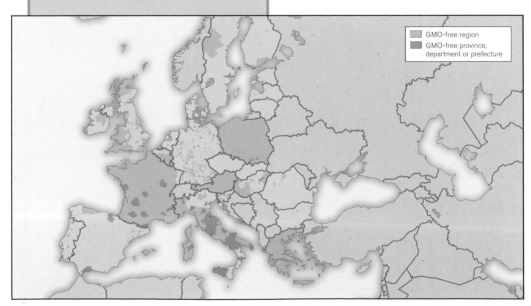

GMO-free region

GMO-free province, department or prefecture

Organic farming

Many, but not all, sustainable farmers also seek to "go organic." This means eliminating the use of all synthetic chemicals in the growing process. But whether organic or not, sustainable farmers try to limit the use of

What would you do?

If you were a farmer, would you choose to accept some added work, such as weeding by hand, so you could grow organic crops? Why or why not?

chemicals. In some cases, they use farming methods of the past. Some farmers plant clover and other crops that return nutrients to the soil. Others weed by hand. To fight pests, some introduce helpful organisms, such as bacteria, or insects that eat harmful pests. Natural products, such as baking soda, can also be used against some insects. Recent studies have shown that organic farming methods can produce about the same yield as industrialized farming does.

Some scientists, however, doubt a switch to completely organic or sustainable farming could meet the world's growing food needs. Nina Federoff, a government scientist in the United States, voiced this view in 2008. She said perhaps only half the world could be fed with strictly organic methods. Either way, organic farming is on the rise (see graph at right to track the recent increase in land that is being farmed organically).

This organic farm produces a variety of vegetables, with some work done by hand.

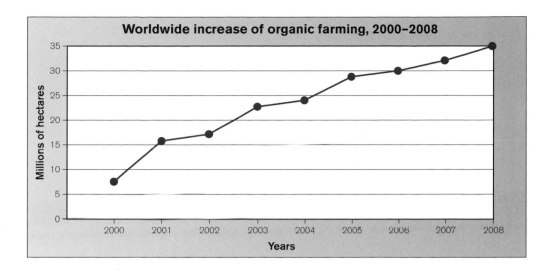

Moreover, a 2007 study from the United Kingdom said organically grown produce may not always be better for the environment. Take tomatoes, for instance. The report said it takes more than 10 times as much land to grow a ton of organic tomatoes, compared to ones grown using chemicals. And producing those organic tomatoes uses about twice as much energy.

The price of organic produce is an issue, too. Organically grown crops are often more expensive than conventionally grown foods. This is partially because these crops can require more labor, and other expenses are often higher for organic farmers.

But any crop can be grown without chemicals. About 10 years ago, Dick and Dora Rochford became certified (government-approved) growers of organic garlic, a crop they had already been raising for years without synthetic fertilizers and pesticides. Garlic has a bad reputation as a smelly vegetable, leading to its nickname—the stinking rose. But its flavor is savored around the world, and garlic has many health benefits. It is known to help lower high blood pressure and fight infection. Through local sales and the Internet, the Rochfords often sell out of their entire crop.

Originally from Ireland, the Rochfords established their farm in Tenterfield, New South Wales, Australia. To add to the international flair, the original source of their Oriental Purple garlic variety was northern China. Like many organic farmers, the Rochfords do not use all of their land each year for growing garlic. In between garlic seasons, they grow clover, which helps add nutrients to the soil. The clover and other crops also provide food for the sheep the Rochfords raise.

Promoters of sustainable and organic farming say the benefits of those methods outweigh the downsides. They also see sustainable farming as part of an effort to connect people to the source of their food. A growing number of people are buying produce at farmers' markets, which feature food from local farmers. The United States saw the number of these markets grow by more than 300 percent between 1994 and 2009.

In the United Kingdom, a national organization called the National Farmers' Retail and Markets Association (FARMA) makes sure the markets have products grown locally and sold by the actual farmers. Whether the produce is organic or not, locally grown crops are considered sustainable. They are not part of the agribusiness system, they are fresher than crops grown far away, and they keep the profits from growing food in the local community. All these concerns are positive elements of the sustainability movement.

"[T]he challenge of food security is best illustrated by the fact that in the next 50 years the global population will consume twice as much food as has ever been consumed since agriculture began 10,000 years ago."
—Clive James, agricultural scientist

Many sustainable farms welcome people to visit and even pick their own crops. This lets people of all ages connect with the farms and farmers that produce much of the food they eat.

Health watch
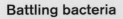
Battling bacteria

In recent years, the spread of E. coli through produce has been a growing concern. E. coli is a bacteria found in cattle that can cause sickness—or even death—in humans. The bacteria can be spread through a cow's manure, with rain or irrigation water carrying it far from the field where it was first found. Farmworkers can also get the E. coli on their boots and spread it as they walk. Outbreaks of E. coli-related illnesses connected to produce, especially leafy greens, have been on the rise in the United States.

Produce from organic farms, though usually considered healthier for consumers than conventionally grown crops, are also at risk of containing E. coli. Cow manure is one of the natural fertilizers used to replace synthetics. Organic farmers have to carefully compost the manure, a process that heats up the manure and kills a variety of harmful bacteria. Waiting up to four months before putting raw manure on a field also reduces the risk of E. coli on organic produce. But in all aspects of agriculture, farmers often can never know if all of their products are 100 percent safe.

Looking ahead

Despite the rise in sustainable agriculture, no one predicts that industrialized farming will end soon. Some agribusinesses sell organic goods and some have switched to sustainable methods. The world's farmers are trying to find a balance between growing enough grains, fruits, and vegetables for all, while doing the least harm to the planet.

The Agricultural Revolution of the past helped end some of the worst extremes of hunger on a global scale. New science and technology aid that effort today. But some people wonder if the industrialized farming that produces so much food creates other problems that people have failed to address.

Providing food security requires balancing many different interests and values. The challenges will increase as populations grow—and, as a recent study suggests, food prices may rise 40 percent in the coming decade. The choices individuals, companies, and governments make will shape the success of meeting the world's food requirements in an ethical way.

Spotlight on Corn

Of all the world's grains, corn might be the one with the most uses. Some people take the seeds, called kernels, and pop them. Others eat the kernels off the long cobs. From a can or frozen container, corn is often served as a side dish, as a vegetable would be. Corn can be ground into a flour, called meal, and used in baking. It goes into feed given to livestock around the world. And it has industrial uses, as products from corn go into such things as fabrics and paper. But one use of corn stirs the most debate: turning it into a sugar called high-fructose corn syrup. Use the chart below to compare the world's primary corn producers.

The world's leading corn producers, 2010	
Country	Thousand metric tons
United States	334,052
China	155,000
EU	56,126
Brazil	51,000
Mexico	22,000
India	18,500
Argentina	15,000
South Africa	11,500
Ukraine	10,500
Canada	9,560

"Hopefully…there will be some effort to step back on the amount of high-fructose corn syrup in our diets."
—Dr. Anthony Heaney, cancer researcher at the University of California at Los Angeles

You've already read about some of the concerns over high-fructose corn syrup. Corn growers and agribusiness companies say it's just another kind of sugar and no different than the white sugar you might put in a cup of tea or use in baking. The syrup also has certain advantages. It's easier to make many food products with high-fructose corn syrup than with solid sugar. The syrup is sweeter and so the companies use less, reducing their costs. Corn syrup also helps keep foods fresher longer when they sit on store shelves. But the corn industry knows high-fructose corn syrup has developed a bad reputation. In 2010, U.S. corn refiners wanted to start using the term "corn sugar" on food labels instead of "high-fructose corn syrup."

Health concerns

Eating too much of any sugar can lead to health problems. But high-fructose corn syrup may present special problems. The results of a study released in 2010 showed that rats gained more weight drinking water containing the syrup than they did drinking an even larger amount of water with table sugar in it. Another study that year suggested that fructose, more than other common sugars, causes a certain kind of cancer to spread.

These studies are small and don't offer definite proof that high-fructose corn syrup is dangerous. But some scientists still study it, while corn growers and refiners defend their product.

Finding sugar in your food

Sometimes it can be difficult to make sense of the ingredients listed on packaged foods. This list shows some of the ingredients you might see listed that are a form of sugar:

Dehydrated cane juice	Maple syrup
Dextrin	Molasses
Dextrose	Raw sugar
Fructose	Rice syrup
Fruit juice concentrate	Saccharose
Glucose	Sorghum or sorghum syrup
Lactose	Sucrose
Maltodextrin	Syrup
Malt syrup	Treacle
Maltose	Xylose

> "There is no nutritional difference between high-fructose corn syrup and sugar. A sugar is a sugar whether it comes from cane, corn, or beets."
> —Audrae Erickson, president of the Corn Refiners Association

Glossary

agribusiness company involved in the large-scale raising and production of food

agriculture raising of crops and animals for food

consumer person who buys goods

crop rotation planting different crops on the same plot of land to help add nutrients to the soil

developing country nation that is building industries and creating more wealth but that is still poorer than the wealthiest nations

domestication process of taking wild plants or animals and taming them for human use

drought long period without rain in a particular region

economy of scale idea that the cost of producing certain goods falls, per each unit, as more of them are produced

edible able to be eaten

environmentalism movement to protect the environment from dangers created by humans

ethics study of good and bad behavior, or a person's own ideas on what is good or bad, right or wrong

famine severe shortage of food in a particular area that leads to many deaths

fertilizer chemical that help crops grow

food security concept of everyone having easy access to affordable, nutritious food

game wild animals hunted for food

genetic engineering changing of an organism's genes so it will develop new traits, often done by adding genes from another organism

genetically modified organism (GMO) animal or plant that has its genes changed, giving it new traits

global warming slow increase in temperatures recorded around the world

greenhouse gas gas that collects above Earth and traps in heat, adding to global warming

harvest to pick fruits, vegetables, or grains when they are ready to be eaten

herbicide chemical that kills weeds or other crop-harming plants

industrialized farming raising crops with the widespread use of machines and science

irrigation system of bringing water to a field where crops are grown

manure animal waste used as a fertilizer

mechanized done by or with the aid of machines

nutrient types of chemicals in foods that are essential for life

organic farming method that does not use chemicals to fertilize crops

organism living creature

pesticide chemical that kills the insects that destroy crops

population total number of people in a given area

process turn a raw crop or animal into a food product

reaper machine that cuts down grain when it's ready to be harvested

refine remove part of a grain to prepare it for use in food

rural far from populated areas; remote

subsidy money given to farmers by a government for raising certain agricultural products

supply and demand notion that the amount produced of a certain item, or the desire people have for it, can go up and down and will make its price change as well

sustainably produced in a way that does the least harm to the environment and humans

synthesized created through scientific effort from existing elements

thresher machine that separates the edible part of a grain from the rest of the plant

yield amount of a certain crop grown in a certain area during a particular time

Further Information

Books

Baines, John D. *Food and Farming*. Mankato, MN: Smart Apple Media, 2009.

Chevat, Richie, and Michael Pollan. *The Omnivore's Dilemma: The Secrets Behind What You Eat*. New York, NY: Dial, 2009.

Kukathas, Uma, ed. *The Global Food Crisis*. Detroit, MI: Greenhaven, 2009.

Langley, Andrew. *Is Organic Food Better?* (*What Do You Think?* series). Chicago, IL: Heinemann Library, 2009.

Mason, Paul. *Food* (*Planet Under Pressure* series). Chicago, IL: Heinemann Library, 2006.

Redlin, Janice L. *Land Abuse and Soil Erosion* (*Understanding Global Issues* series). New York, NY: Weigl, 2007.

Spilsbury, Richard, and Louise Spilsbury. *From Farm to Table* (*Food and Farming* series). New York, NY: PowerKids, 2011.

Websites

www.fao.org
The website of the Food and Agriculture Organization of the United Nations looks at food security and hunger from a global perspective, with statistics on food production from around the world.

www.sustainabletable.org
The Sustainable Table website was created by a group dedicated to sustainable agriculture. The site includes useful tips on where to find sustainable products.

www.usda.gov
The official U.S. Department of Agriculture site has the latest news on farming in the United States, a history of U.S. agriculture, and information on such topics as soils and food safety.

www.wholegrainscouncil.org
This U.S.-based Whole Grains Council is an organization that promotes the use of whole grains that have not been processed, and therefore contain more nutrients.

http://ec.europa.eu/agriculture/publi/capexplained/cap_en.pdf
This document from the European Union (EU) explains the goals of the Common Agricultural Policy (CAP) and also offers a look at the role EU farmers play in world agricultural trade.

Topics for further research

All crops need water to grow. As you read on page 16, one solution for growing crops where water is scarce is hydroponics. How does this method work? Where has it been used?

What are the main grains and vegetables produced in your country? Which ones, if any, are sold overseas in large amounts?

Many people who grow their own vegetables use compost as a natural fertilizer. What is compost, and how is it made?

Rice, like corn, can be found in a variety of products. What are some of these products? What are the nutritional differences between brown and white rice? What countries lead the world in rice production and consumption?

Index